"By the grace of God I am what I am, and his grace toward me has not been in vain."
(1 Corinthians 15:10)

Touched By Grace Ministry
#drbondhopson and other social media addresses

DR. CYNTHIA A. BOND HOPSON

TOTALLY
grace
FULL

wisdom for
phenomenal
& grace-filled
women

innovo
PUBLISHING

Published by Innovo Publishing, LLC
www.innovopublishing.com
1-888-546-2111

innovo
PUBLISHING

Providing Full-Service Publishing Services for Christian Authors,
Artists & Ministries:
Books, eBooks, Audiobooks, Music, Film & Courses

TOTALLY GRACEFULL
Wisdom for Phenomenal & Grace-Filled Women

Library of Congress Control Number: 2018963389
ISBN: 978-1-61314-461-9

Cover Design & Interior Layout: Innovo Publishing, LLC

Printed in the United States of America
U.S. Printing History
First Edition: 2019

Contents

Acknowledgments

Totally Gracefull is humbly dedicated to God. God and I have been friends for longer than I can remember. I've had, and I have, a blessed life—four wonderful parents, siblings, cousins, nieces and nephews, aunts and uncles—then a great husband, amazing children, cute and smart grandchildren, sweet great-grandson, Avery, supportive and precious in-laws, and Crystal—just the most phenomenal village ever. I have incredible friends—they challenge and bless me in all the ways I need (WOW!), and the best is yet to come!

I am grateful for every hug, every sweet note and email, "you working on a book?" question, the United Methodist Women, every Facebook and Twitter follower—I'll never get finished naming all the ways and people who have touched my life and keep pushing me way past the exit I've chosen. Wherever you are, thank you. I am humbled and so eternally grateful for those of you who prayed for and with me, for those who will read these pages and be inspired to start, to walk, to speak, to finish, to conquer—not because of me but because God is ordering our steps.

I owe the honesty team: Tammy, Debbie, Linda, Sophia— the God-fearing women who said to go forth and watch God do what only God can do. To Roger, who's always in my corner cheering me on. To Leah for Bart, Rachael, and Yvonne. To Nicole who is always ready. For my mother, Miss Marie, who always makes me want to act in a way that makes her proud. For my children, siblings, in-laws and their families, for all those who love justice and work for it daily, and for those who encourage and support righteousness in every place: *Thank you.*

Be blessed, and keep shining!

Foreword

The great sage, author, poet, and activist Dr. Maya Angelou is known for many wise words. One lesson she often shared is this: "I've learned that people will forget what you said, people will forget what you did, but people will never forget how you made them feel." If you ever encounter Dr. Cynthia A. Bond Hopson, you will never forget any of those things.

Around 2007, one of my dear colleagues introduced me to Dr. Hopson to help facilitate and manage a work project. Our positive kindred spirits immediately connected. Soon after, Dr. Hopson came to me to help promote the services of her ministry, Touched by Grace, which inspires and empowers people to live faithfully and triumphantly. Because her presence had already been inspiring to me, I had to say, "Yes." With steady and strategic plodding, my marketing team worked to create the brand for Touched by Grace and position it on digital media platforms. We carefully created imagery, language, and products to honor God's grace upon Dr. Hopson, so that she could expand her opportunities to be a blessing to others.

Over the years, I grew to affectionately call her "Sunshine" because that is what she embodies; she affectionately calls me the same, along with "Precious" and other loving pet names. I learned that when she leads a sentence with "Precious," I should expect something impactful—and more work—to follow. During one of our regular strategic planning meetings, that's exactly what she did. "Precious," she said, in her infectious and commanding voice. She went on to describe her vision to write a series of uplifting messages, similar to her days of writing a regular column for her local newspaper. We birthed the monthly e-newsletter, *Gracefull: Words of Wisdom for Phenomenal and Grace-Filled Women.*

The response was overwhelmingly positive and heart-warming. Her audience was grateful to receive regular messages that were so uplifting, and we were grateful to be used by God to deliver them. We grew the e-newsletter into what is now the weekly *Gracefull* blog and connected it to her new website. We used the sentiment of Dr. Hopson's blog followers to create the new website tagline: *Uplifting, Engaging, Inspiring*. And we know that this compilation of Dr. Hopson's favorite *Gracefull* blogs will do just that—uplift, engage, and inspire each reader to live triumphantly into their grace-filled life.

An African proverb reminds us that it takes a village to raise a child; we feel like godparents to *Totally Gracefull*, and it has taken a village to raise her. Our team members, Rick, Peg, Korina, Faith, Diandria, Sowmya, Kris, and so many others, have been blessed and honored to be a part of Dr. Hopson's journey. Though I have transitioned to another business service offering, I have kept Dr. Hopson as my one-and-only strategic marketing client because I believe in her work and the impact she is making one person at a time. She has proclaimed herself as the chief inspiration officer, and I would agree.

After reading *Totally Gracefull*, I submit that you won't forget what Dr. Hopson said, what she did, and most assuredly, you will *never* forget how she made you feel.

—**Kimberlee Scott**
Chief Marketing Strategist,
KAI Strategic Marketing Group

Preface

*W*elcome to *Totally Gracefull*. It is a gift from God, and I am thankful for the opportunity to share it with you.

What in the world is *Totally Gracefull*? I'm delighted you asked. And to answer this question, I need to start from the beginning . . .

I finished my doctoral degree in 2000 after seven years, nine months, twenty-one days, and four hours. To say I was exhausted and scarred is putting it mildly, but I immediately began trying to decide how to share the lessons and be a blessing. In 2002, God blessed me with Touched By Grace, an anointed ministry for women that helped me focus on my writing, training, and speaking instead of trying to be all things to all people. God inspired the name *Gracefull* and the scriptural reference (1 Corinthians 15:10) and offered opportunities galore to spread His message of love, forgiveness, enthusiasm, and grace. Eight books, forty-nine states, and six continents later, I've only just begun!

In the fall of 2010, *Gracefull*, the newsletter, emerged. Like me, this newsletter had humble beginnings. It started as a way for me to keep in touch with my followers and friends. From the first issue, the response was enthusiastic, affirmative, and divine confirmation that if I would hold still and be a vehicle for joy, God would do the rest. As the *Gracefull* newsletter evolved into *Gracefull* the blog, Kimberlee Scott and her KAI Strategic Marketing and Aephephani teams obeyed God and moved this ministry to the next level. They work around the clock to keep me and you fresh, inspired, and poised to do God's bidding. *Gracefull* has now evolved into a weekly offering designed to scatter "sunshine," as my friend Martha calls it, to grace-filled and phenomenal women everywhere.

Here is some fuel from my email archives:

> "Thank you for your ministry through Touched By Grace. The inspiration and challenges provide encouragement and support for the journey."

"What a wonderful treat to wake this morning and stumble into the den with my coffee and find YOU on the computer. YOU, my friend, are amazing and scatter sunshine on a gloomy day. Thanks for the newsletter. It will make my day so much brighter."

"Thanks so much for the inspiring words of wisdom. You are a gifted writer who has richly blessed me!"

"You are so loved and appreciated. I praise God for your spirit of encouragement."

"Touched By Grace Ministry just made my day, Tuesday morning, 8:51 a.m. Keep up this ministry, and may the Lord continue to strengthen you to encourage others, especially one like me. You have certainly inspired me to get a grip on things and do better in taking care of ME and my health. You are absolutely amazing and incredibly incredible!!!!!!!!!! CONTINUE!"

"LUV IT!!!!!!!!!!!!! Wonderful reminders and information that motivates and encourages even this 'old head.' I will be forwarding it to all my friends and family. I look forward to the next issue. Yeah, Cynthia!"

"This is really great. I read and receive your words of encouragement."

How to Use this Book

What you have in your li'l warm hands is a collection of my favorite *Gracefull* entries—*Totally Gracefull.* There are 31 reflections, to be precise—one for each day of the month. If you read four or five at a time, you won't be turned into a pumpkin or zapped by ninja turtles! Keep *Totally Gracefull* by your bedside or in your purse, share it with a friend, or do all of the above, wherever/whenever you need inspiration and a smile. I pray you'll spend this special time with me and God and be gently reminded that you are absolutely full of grace, hope, and love.

Whenever I try to describe women of God, I usually rely on Proverbs 31. When I read it, I smile and then I get tired! This sister is up early, she's busy all day, here and there, but verse 29 tells the real rest of the story. The words vary about what she has done, but the gist is that lots of women have done "excellently," "nobly," "worthily," "wonderfully," "great things"—there are as many different words as translations and versions—but verse 29 is the official "drop the mic"[1] moment. It translates to the fact that "tons of folks have done some amazing things and accomplished incredible feats, but *you*, my dear, surpass them all!" That's all I'm saying to you today: *You have surpassed them all!* I pray that through this time and space, you will acknowledge and bask in your own beauty, magnificence, power, and grace. When you stop and think about it, you have been created in the image of God, and that means you are limitless, unconquerable, dynamic, and amazing—to infinity and back!

As you keep being your li'l phenomenal selves today, doing what you do—knocking at and kicking down doors, and making the way by walking it—remember to take some time and just *be*. *Be* still. *Be* joyful. *Be* at peace. *Be* thankful. *Be* powerful, and cover all the ground you're standing on. Lend a ladder, a leg, a hand, and a heart. *Be* God's woman, full of grace and wisdom—God's handiwork, God's proudest moment. *Be* proud of who and where you are, where you've been—scars and all— and then *spread your wings and soar!*

—Cynthia

---

1. "Drop the mic": According to Wikipedia, "A mic drop is the gesture of intentionally dropping one's microphone at the end of a performance or speech to signal triumph. Figuratively, it is an expression of triumph for a successful event and indicates a boastful attitude toward one's own performance." (en.wikipedia.org/wiki/Mic_drop)

Official Gracefull
To-Do List

I am a firm believer in to-do lists because they offer an intentional roadmap for your day. I get twice as much done and I feel like a million bucks when my to-do list is finished! I put everyday stuff on there (vacuuming, loading the dishwasher, making the bed, etc.) so I can triumphantly cross mundane things off too. The list below has fun and important stuff on it, so pick your favorites and get busy . . .

- Treat yourself to a Sunday afternoon nap this weekend. It is a luxury you definitely deserve!

- Put all your change in a designated place from now until Thanksgiving Day. Then count it, give half to charity, and blow the rest on something memorable.

- Next summer, go one place you've been meaning to but haven't yet.

- Adopt a "No Excuses" policy. Don't accept excuses from others or yourself. Prepare for excellence in every way—don't even think of leaving the house without looking your best. Presume you're going to meet your idol and you want their response to be, "Wow, you are looking some kind of fabulous, Miss Lady! They created the word *stunning* just for you!" And, yes, they did!

- For the next two weeks, leave home eleven minutes earlier than usual for appointments. (Nothing magical or mysterious about eleven—it just sounds way cooler than ten!)

- Deliberately bless someone today—sponsor lunch, send a note, give a compliment, fill in the _____.

- Starting Monday, gather your old photos, and date and identify them. Scan them into your computer, or get them put on a disk to preserve them.

- Be real clear: if you keep doing what you've been doing, you will absolutely, positively keep getting what you've been getting—I'm just sayin'.

1

"Nothing Is Worth More Than This Day."

(Goethe)

oday is the day. I will step out on faith. I will do that thing I've been afraid to do.

I'd been waiting on a sign—like Moses had when he was walking along and came upon a bush that was burning but not consumed. God said, "Remove the sandals from your feet, for the place on which you are standing is holy ground" (Exodus 3:5). That, I could imagine and understand. Or when Jesus was getting baptized, and a voice from heaven boomed: "This is my Son, the Beloved, with whom I am well pleased" (Matthew 3:17). This I could also understand, so I kept waiting for a holy shoe, some smoke, a roar of thunder, something—anything—that might move me forward. I finally realized that God was getting my attention, but through quiet, subtle ways. Here's what I heard:

> ❧ *"Spread your wings; I will do the rest!"* I did the Gallup StrengthsFinder survey[2] recently, and it helped me discover what I'm really good at. As usual, there were no surprises, but I was still reluctant to soar without a charred bush or two. God and my coach, Meagan, gently

---

2. www.gallupstrengthscenter.com

reminded me that I had to trust my faith and boldly step out—actually practice what I'd been preaching. Meagan said, "You've been preparing long enough—maybe *you're* calling *you*" to follow your dreams and be audacious *and* bodacious. She said, "Exploit your strengths and the things you're confident about." So today I'm ready to conquer and soar!

ᔥ *"Humility and kindness matter."* I was listening to Country radio and superstar Tim McGraw's "Humble and Kind," and the lyrics whispered,

I know you got mountains to climb
but always stay humble and kind.
When those dreams you're dreamin' come to you,
when the work you put in is realized,
let yourself feel the pride
but always stay humble and kind.
When you get where you're going
don't forget to turn back around and help the next one in line
and always be humble and kind.

I thought about all the people (like you) who pray for, believe in, and encourage me daily, and I know when we do this for each other, there's no limit to what we can do and where we can go. So today, remember to care for and encourage someone, and always be humble and kind.

ᔥ *"Refuse to live with fear,"* for it will paralyze you, and much of what you have been called to do won't and can't be done. Listen for God's whisper—it serves the same purpose as burning bushes and holy shoes. Trust God and your heart for direction—wherever you're going, God is already there. Be courageous, and live mightily, for today is yours. Make it count!

Now that you mention it, I will/could/might/won't …

Use the space below to jot down some reflections after this reading.

_____

_____

_____

_____

_____

_____

_____

_____

_____

2

The Best Advice I Ever Took

'm just full of good advice these days. How do I know all this stuff? Because I'm in my midsixties, I've been reading *Dear Abby* for fifty-plus years, and I try to listen and learn from every experience. I read a recent article about some powerful women. They were asked, "What's the best piece of advice you've ever gotten?" I thought about it, and here are some of my favorites:

1. *You have two ears and one mouth for a purpose.* Listen twice as much as you speak, and know that once the words have been spoken, you can't unspeak them.

2. *No amount of money can buy time, courage, or integrity.* A bigger house, a faster car, and more stuff, yes; but time, courage, and integrity are what make life worthwhile.

3. *Refuse to live with regret.* The stakes are too high for you to put off things that matter. Stop making excuses and write that book, take that trip, go to that class reunion, send that note—and do it today.

4. *You never get a second chance to make a good first impression.* Aim for stunning *every time*, and the rest is easy! Don't run to the store at 2 a.m. looking like a hot, sizzling mess because everybody else has the same plan. Presume you will (a) get discovered by some talent agent, (b) meet

your boss, or (c) meet your new significant other while you're there. So be prepared for excellence, and if you don't see anybody you know, count it all joy!

5. *To save time, take time to do it right the first time.* I can hear my grandmother saying, "If you can't find time to do it right, how will you find time to do it over?" Do your best every time—it'll make all the difference.

6. *The way you treat you is the way others will treat you.* Carry yourself proudly. Expect respect, and give it in equal measures. Dignity and enthusiasm are at the heart of greatness. Live like you know it!

7. *Give, spend, and save* your money, your time, and your resources, and you will always have plenty.

8. *Laugh often,* treasure your friends, and make time for them. Every day!

9. *Have your own stuff, especially your own money!* Whatever you will need, make sure you have your own so you won't have to beg, borrow, or steal.

Now that you mention it, I will/could/might/won't . . .

Use the space below to jot down some reflections after this reading.

_____

_____

_____

_____

_____

_____

_____

3

Live Until You Die & Then Die Boldly!

I loved and admired Dr. Johnetta Walker Neal, and I told her so often. I'm so glad I did, because she died unexpectedly not much more than a week after I saw her last. She participated in the Fourth Annual Phenomenal Women Speak community event in Brownsville, TN, and I poured it on extra thick in the mushy note I included in her gift bag. Her response to me, "You're a real star," made me feel ten feet tall and as rich as Oprah *and* Bill and Melinda Gates!

I was the proud president and CEO of her fan club, and she knew it. She was always elegant and sophisticated, and I *never* heard her be angry, mean, or unkind. When she wore coverings on her head, she looked stunning and regal. I, on the other hand, looked like four months of hard winter.

I don't recall a time when she wasn't part of my life. In my earliest remembrances from church and family gatherings (we were cousins), she always treated me like a person of great worth and not some bratty nuisance. She intentionally encouraged and included me in everything and gently nudged me to stay focused and keep moving ahead. As I have gotten older, I know how important this is for children and others who too often get overlooked or banished to a corner to be seen and not heard.

I'm sharing her with you today because I want to be like her when I grow up. I want to lift, empower, inspire, reach out and up—be a lantern and a ladder, as one writer said—be a beacon of light and hope like Jesus, and help someone go North, as Johnetta so powerfully put it (escaped slaves were encouraged to follow the North Star to freedom and not to give up or turn back when the going got tough). She was a loving wife and soulmate to Rowan for forty-eight years and one week, a doting mom, grandmother, sister, cousin, aunt, activist, and friend, and she was most excellent in each role.

As you help me bask in Johnetta's amazing life, let's plan to live our own with passion, grace, patience, courage, purpose, and integrity. Here's why:

- No matter what kind of life we live, someone's going to want to be like us. Let's leave a beautiful and extraordinary example to follow.

- Kindness and intentional care are the common denominators in relationships. When we lend a hand or offer an encouraging word or genuine interest, it poignantly reminds us that we are all important in the sight of God.

- Showing up and being/having a non-anxious but essential presence should be our daily goal. "Keep calm and carry on" is an old British slogan, but it's a good word for today and an even more excellent way to live a life of service every day.

- Honesty and integrity always matter, and what we do in private has to match what we show the world. That means we keep our word, we lift as we climb, we go out of our way to make a difference, and when our time comes to go, we rejoice and give thanks for the journey. *Amen.*

Now that you mention it, I will/could/might/won't ...
Use the space below to jot down some reflections after this reading.

_____

_____

_____

_____

_____

_____

_____

_____

_____

4

"The More Things Change, the More You Grow."

(Reba McEntire)

*I*f this is true—and in my case, it seems to be—I am growing like the national debt! Every way I turn, something is moving, shifting, being tossed about, becoming unsettled or unsteady, causing concern . . . you get the picture. I don't remember asking God for this particular growth spurt, yet here I am, just growinnnnnnnnnnng.

I handle change pretty well as long as I have warning, preparation, and some better place to be at the end of it. There, I said it—but we know that saying it and actually changing are not the same thing. When you decide to have a child, move, change jobs, or change marital status—you are making a conscious choice. Don't worry, I'm still happily married to Roger Dodger, have a job, and don't know anything about birthing babies at retirement age, but Roger and I are moving. I am excited about new possibilities, and I'm feverishly packing boxes and getting our house ready for sale. So, what am I feeling? Uncertainty, off-kilter, excited—depends on the day!

During this time of change, it seems every week there are at least two or three funerals to attend. (And these folks were about my age, so they were dying young!) *And,* my great new interim boss of less than two months had a heart attack and died. The one before him stayed only nine months. Of course, with every new boss you have to start all over, proving you have good sense. We were just discovering how to work together when he died suddenly.

Therefore, I'm praying that this relocation will be uneventful. Roger assumed a pastorate on July 1, 2017, so we now have parishioners and are at the same place every Sunday.[3] Though we are calling it adventure, nevertheless, *everything is changing!*

I don't know what's going on with you—maybe lots of change or none at all. But here are two things I do know:

1. *Even when you can't see or understand what God is doing, God has a plan.* Jeremiah 29:11 says the plan is to give you "welfare and not . . . harm, to give you a future with hope." We can trust God with what comes next—with the details, both large and small. And the beautiful thing here is that nothing will happen today that God doesn't know about and isn't working out for our good. So whether I'm excited or a tad anxious, I am confident that God loves me and keeps blessing me in a magnificent way.

2. *You can't put stuff off—life is uncertain and fragile.* Do it today— whatever *it* is. Write that note; go see your Aunt Florence while she can still enjoy a visit. Forgive—anybody, everybody, yourself. Period. Go on a cruise or to your class reunion and have a ball. Don't worry about the gray hair and the size 16W. Trust me, you will be looking great for your age! Register for those missing classes and finish your degree. Make a plan to move forward. Remember, change is good, especially when you get to direct and control it.

Today, take time to admire the sunrise and sunset, and be in awe of the beautiful flowers, trees, and clouds. Bask in God's grace and mercy. Join in the laughter of happy children. Be kind. And remember, change is growth; so count it all joy! *Amen.*

---

3. Roger and I are having a ball being the pastor and "pastor's wife," as Miss Lorene calls me, of the Centenary United Methodist Church, 584 E McLemore Ave, Memphis, TN 38106. Worship starts promptly at 8 and 10:30 a.m. Please plan to join us soon.

Now that you mention it, I will/could/might/won't . . .

Use the space below to jot down some reflections after this reading.

_____

_____

_____

_____

_____

_____

_____

_____

_____

5

Thank You, Sister Maya

I didn't get to know Dr. Maya Angelou personally, but that didn't stop her from blessing my life. I never got to tell her how much her work had meant throughout my life and my uncertainties. I never had the chance to sit at her feet and have her help me find the incredible "me" still lurking inside. Yet I know I am wiser, richer, and more phenomenal because of her life and words. We all are.

The powerful lessons Sister Maya taught through living and sharing her amazing life powerfully offer a rich tapestry of introspection for us womenfolk. Where are we? What are we doing with our voices? What can we teach and learn today that will make our lives and the world richer, more peaceful, less confusing, and worth the while? Her wise words are all around us, but here are four of my favorite passages:

> *"Perhaps travel cannot prevent bigotry, but by demonstrating that all peoples cry, laugh, eat, worry, and die, it can introduce the idea that if we try and understand each other, we may even become friends."* As women, we must become more aware of ourselves and the world around us. We are powerful, smart, and important, and we have something to say (about almost everything). We must flex our collective strength, clout, and interest, or our humanity goes to hell in a handbasket. I've seen poverty and hopelessness

from Rio de Janeiro to Appalachia, from the school cafeteria to the dusty, hollow-eyed sisters on the streets, and they look the same. We must see, hear, and understand each other for God's sake.

✺ *"Be a rainbow in someone's cloud."* I saw two rainbows on Tuesday, and I praised God for the gentle reminder that, in my words and deeds, I can be the difference between lifting up and tearing down. It took me a while to discover my "call," but once I got it, *I got it*. It's spreading sunshine—almost the same thing as being a rainbow, since you can get both after the rain. Today, don't miss your chance to roll away some clouds.

✺ *"You are the sum total of everything you've ever seen, heard, eaten, smelled, been told, forgot—it's all there. Everything influences each of us, and because of that I try to make sure that my experiences are positive."* Confucius puts it this way: "If I am walking with two other men, each of them will serve as my teacher. I will pick out the good points of the one and imitate them and the bad points of the other and correct them in myself." I call it my "Mrs. Potato Head Syndrome." I took up the positives from some of my favorite people over the years and did my darndest to leave behind what my mother called my "ugly ways." Whether it's punctuality, my love for beautiful jewelry, fragrances, and compelling books, or how I carry myself, Confucius and Dr. Angelou are right. Every day we get a new opportunity to reinvent ourselves. Certainly it's not so simplistic as deciding, but specifically making the decision to change, to improve, and to soar is absolutely a great start.

✺ *"One isn't necessarily born with courage, but one is born with potential. Without courage, we cannot practice any other virtue with consistency. We can't be kind, true, merciful, generous, or honest."* Enough said.

Amen.

Now that you mention it, I will/could/might/won't …
Use the space below to jot down some reflections after this reading.

_____

_____

_____

_____

_____

_____

_____

_____

6

Let There Be Peace on Earth, and Let It Begin with Me

I promise you, my middle name is not Pollyanna,[4] but today I am pledging to not just imagine a world where there is no hatred and strife—I'm pledging to remember and live out the words of diarist Anne Frank and repeat them daily: "In spite of everything, I still believe that people are really good at heart."

As we look around at the confusion and chaos swirling in our world, sometimes it's difficult to remember that people are good. When there are school shootings almost every week, suicide bombings, massacres like in Las Vegas where fifty-nine innocent people died and more than five hundred were injured, and there is senseless violence at restaurants, theaters, and on sidewalks, a twenty-four-hour news cycle filled with hate-generated conversations, and there are rowdies who wreak havoc and loot instead of peacefully marching to protest violence—something must change, and soon. Couple that with natural disasters like catastrophic storms, earthquakes, fires,

---

4. Pollyanna is a fictitious character from a book of the same name and is described as someone whose forever sunny disposition often works the nerves of those around her.

floods, and droughts—I don't know about you, but I'm simply overwhelmed.

Staying at home with the covers pulled up over our heads may sound like a solution, but the place in which we find ourselves today calls for action and these gentle reminders:

1. *"God did not give us a spirit of cowardice, but rather a spirit of power and of love and of self-discipline" (2 Timothy 1:7). Act like it.* Live until you die! Be vigilant and pay attention, but refuse to be governed by *fear!* I applaud those who jump right into action, caring for others, binding up wounds, saving lives—doing what comes naturally—even putting themselves in harm's way. We call them heroes, but they are ordinary people who do extraordinary things in times of challenge. I pray that when it is our turn, we, too, will step up and be the difference.

2. *Stop wringing your hands, and use them to create change.* At first, the attacks on innocents, the terrorist rumblings, and the subtle discrimination and intolerance seemed far away. Either I didn't know the people involved or it wasn't my issue that day, but now when we ignore the things swirling around us, we do so at our own peril. If we're not careful, fear and neglect will govern everything we do—who we associate with, what we fight for, where we go, who and what we value—and then the only thing left will be chaos and confusion.

   Make phone calls and send emails on important topics to your elected officials. Become an advocate for change. Whether it's healthcare, affordable housing, homelessness, gun control, immigration, right to life, capital punishment—all are quality of life matters for us and our neighbors. Stand up, speak up, roll up your sleeves, and be counted and counted on.

3. *Be patient with and deliberately interested in others. Offer an encouraging word, and love everyone like Jesus does.* So many issues we deal with have long-term effects and may be invisible. The mental health of war and storm survivors is something we might overlook if we're not careful. My friends, we must pray for the mental well-being of our

neighbors and friends. These invisible and silent wounds will be more prevalent as the massacres and disasters continue to permeate our world. Don't just avoid the woman down the street who wanders aimlessly, talking to herself, or the children who still suffer from nightmares because they saw their parents or siblings beaten or murdered. The scars may be hidden under our clothes and behind our smiling eyes, but if we take time to listen to the stories, we will know the suffering didn't end when the debris was hauled away and the deployments ended. Sit a spell, hold a hand, pass a tissue—whatever "being there" looks like, let's do it, for heaven's sake. *Amen.*

Now that you mention it, I will/could/might/won't . . .

Use the space below to jot down some reflections after this reading.

_____

_____

_____

_____

_____

_____

_____

_____

_____

7

I Will Trust in the Lord

"Either I'm going to trust you or I may as well walk away. 'Cause stressing . . . don't make it better, no way."[5]

I didn't write the lyrics to Erica Campbell's hit song "Yesterday," but I (a) could have, because last month I was overwhelmed and unsettled in every phase and place; (b) should have, since I had poignant illustrations that would have made a perfect country song; (c) didn't need to write a song because I was over half finished eating an elephant[6] for lunch (with mustard, pickles, and onions) yesterday when I finally realized why I had a stomachache the size of Texas! I had bitten off a lot more than I could chew, and there was nowhere to spit it out!

Here are two things I had to learn the haaaaaard way:

1. *When you're trying to run your own life, no matter how big or old you are, you are in over your head! Ask for help*—again and again, if needed, and understand that God's timing is perfect; yours isn't. I was praying and asking God to help me handle things I wouldn't let go of. God wants our adoration and obedience, not our excuses and explanations.

---

5. Lyrics from "Yesterday" by Erica Atkins-Campbell.
6. Fret not. No animals were harmed in the making of this sandwich (or book)!

2. *There is value in the valley, and blessings come from the lessons.* According to relationship guru Iyanla Van Zant, if you find yourself in a difficult place—a valley-kinda place—she says to be still, because sometimes we are so busy trying to get out of our dark places that we often miss the lessons and the blessings.

I hate it when Sister Van Zant talks directly to me, but as usual, she's right. Moving my household this year has been a valley for me. By its very nature, moving is stressful, but I underestimated what it takes to sell a house—packing, staging, decluttering, cleaning, etc., finding and buying a house, and moving while working full time and commuting three and a half hours on the weekend. In the past when we've moved, we knew when and where we were going and how long our usual stuff would need to be packed up—all things I could control. This time we're dependent on variables out of my control.

Nevertheless, I know now that this unsettling feeling is God's gentle reminder that there is very little I am controlling or in charge of anyway! Like the song says, "Without Him, I could do nothing."[7] It's true. Everywhere I've been, God has been there when I arrived, opening doors and putting out the welcome mat. God has always provided, so why am I fretting? Why am I stressing? The lesson for today is simple: God knows the plans He has for me—plans to prosper me and give me a future with hope (Jeremiah 29:11). These are words you and I can trust completely.

Your dark place, your valley, your unsettled place today may be totally different. It may be opioid addiction, uncertainty, abuse, homelessness, hopelessness, job loss—I don't know, but wherever you are, God is there to remind you that we go through the valley for a reason and a season—we don't stay there. If you're in the valley, God is right there beside you, cheering you on, holding you up, and protecting you. Delight yourself in this blessed assurance! *Amen.*

---

7. Mylon LeFevre, "Without Him."

Now that you mention it, I will/could/might/won't . . .
Use the space below to jot down some reflections after this reading.

_____

_____

_____

_____

_____

_____

_____

_____

8

"You Are Never Too Old to Set Another Goal or to Dream a New Dream."

(C. S. Lewis)

"I have an announcement to make. Frosty the Snowman is a fake, and I don't like him," my three-year-old niece, London, announced at Christmas Eve dinner at my house one year.

All of us around the table were stunned at this news and dissolved into side-splitting laughter. Even now as I recall her oh-so-serious declaration, I'm smiling. I still don't know what Frosty did to get on London's bad side, but he (or somebody) has got some "splaining" to do!

Like London, I, too, have an announcement: *We are only as amazing and powerful as our most bodacious dreams!* Whether we're dreaming of the perfect job, a dream home, or making some life-saving technological or medical discovery, we can't just dream it; we must invest in it and eat, sleep, and breathe it. *We must own it* in every way!

If your dreams aren't keeping you awake or distracting you from your dailiness, are they really worthy of your time and energy? When I was growing up in rural West Tennessee, my dreams of being a fashion model or a San Francisco private detective immediately whisked me away from the endless rows of cotton, okra, and squash. I could see myself wearing the beautiful clothes, driving a sporty convertible, and helping that cute Perry Mason solve crimes. (I took full advantage of the three official television channels we had and never complained that there was nothing on!) I wouldn't have made it without my dreams!

The powerful quote above from C. S. Lewis is a poignant reminder that dreams are an important part of who we are and how we live our lives. Dreams fuel our future, provide a respite from daily doldrums, and give God some special quiet time with us. Jeremiah 29:11 reminds us that God has big plans for us—plans to prosper us and give us a future with hope. I believe dreams help us know and listen to God's heart.

Take a look at where you are today:

- *Are you living into your dreams?* It's easy to daydream during meetings and plan what your life could look like, but when you wake up, are you taking concrete steps to live faithfully? Does what you're doing inspire the rest of us? Does your life help us to imagine our own possibilities? Are you challenging us to learn more, to be, know, and want more—not more stuff but more personal fulfillment, more meaning to what we do?

- *When was the last time you dreamed something so bodacious and scary you had to bring out your "A" game?* I believe that Robert Kiyosaki's right: "The size of your success is measured by the strength of your desire; the size of your dream; and how you handle disappointment along the way."

In business, competition is good; when a new hotel comes to town, their competitors discard the worn chairs, scratchy towels, and dingy carpets to enhance their curb appeal. Dreams are much the same way: if they're not big and bold enough, the quote from the movie *The Lion King* jolts us out of our complacency: "You are more than what you have become."

Fear of failure, lack of trust, and shaky faith are all dream busters. Today we can choose to wallow in fear or walk by faith. Which will you choose? *Amen.*

Now that you mention it, I will/could/might/won't . . .
Use the space below to jot down some reflections after this reading.

_____

_____

_____

_____

_____

_____

_____

_____

_____

9

The Two Most Powerful Words in the Dictionary

*S*even years, nine months, twenty-one days. That's how long it took me to start and finish my doctoral degree. Sometimes eleven hundred miles a week to and from work, classes, and home. A dissertation committee with different opinions about what needed to be included/excluded/inserted/cut/shared/not shared.

When I wanted to make a U-turn in the middle of the street and never return to class, those two words "don't quit" haunted me as surely as the ghosts of Christmases past/present/future plagued Ebenezer Scrooge. When I stayed up all day, all night, and all day again trying to get my statistical equations to make sense, I heard, "don't quit."

Today I am telling you that these two words, plus the other 196 that follow in the poem below, may be more important and powerful than smarts, good looks, status, a really cool car, or a fancy job title. I believe they may mean the difference between victory and defeat, giving up or going forward, hope and utter despair.

It's been eighteen years since I finished my degree and happily added those three letters (PhD) after my name, but

I am confident that this poem and the simplified version my Grandma Clara always quoted ("If a task is once begun, never leave it 'til it's done. Be the labor great or small, do it well or not at all") helped me get there.

Don't Quit

When things go wrong, as they sometimes will,
When the road you're trudging seems all uphill,
When the funds are low and the debts are high,
And you want to smile, but you have to sigh,
When care is pressing you down a bit—
Rest if you must, but don't you quit.

Life is queer with its twists and turns,
As every one of us sometimes learns,
And many a fellow turns about
When he might have won had he stuck it out.
Don't give up though the pace seems slow—
You may succeed with another blow.

Often the goal is nearer than
It seems to a faint and faltering man;
Often the struggler has given up
When he might have captured the victor's cup;
And he learned too late when the night came down,
How close he was to the golden crown.

Success is failure turned inside out—
The silver tint in the clouds of doubt,
And you never can tell how close you are,
It might be near when it seems afar;
So stick to the fight when you're hardest hit—
It's when things seem worst that you must not quit.

I'm not sure who the "Don't Quit" poet is, but here's what I've learned:

> ❧ *Passion, perseverance, and purpose are always more powerful than difficulty.* Whether you're building a house, a career, or a life, be totally committed to your ideals and dreams. There are no perfect plans, but have faith and at least a well-thought-out plan A.

> ❧ *Listen to the experts and learn from their mistakes, and be willing to make some of your own and learn from them too.* Mistakes + time = experience. Have a self-imposed deadline and keep it—come hail or high water.

> ❧ *Begin. You can't finish if you don't start.* A final word from former UN General Secretary Dag Hammarskjold: "Never measure the height of a mountain until you have reached the top. Then you will see how low it was." Build as much success into your process as possible to improve your chances of completing what you start.

Now that you mention it, I will/could/might/won't . . .

Use the space below to jot down some reflections after this reading.

_____

_____

_____

_____

_____

_____

_____

_____

10

You Are Amazing & Incredibly Incredible!

*H*appy winter and a very fine hallelujah to the new year too! The amazing and incredible ones are on their way to a new year in a *big* way! *Oh yeah!* For some reason we often take our li'l, fabulous selves for granted and forget how amazing we really are.

We are more than a collection of breasts, hips, legs, arms, teeth, and ears assembled and packaged into somebody's sister, wife, "woman," mother, grandmother, cousin, aunt, or employee. God has created and called us to be more, and this new year is an excellent time to go ahead and let God finish the great work that has been begun in us!

I am a real sucker for *Undercover Boss*, the reality show where company bosses, you guessed it, go undercover to see the *real* folks at work. In every episode they see what could be improved and eventually give nice gifts and vacations to the unsuspecting employees. The thing I love most, though, is that the bosses actually *see* their employees and hear their stories.

One employee told her CEO afterwards, "This is the first time anyone's ever said I'm amazing!" Today I remind you: You *are* amazing and incredible. Think about where you are, where you've been, what you've accomplished, and what could've, should've, might've happened but didn't, and celebrate the journey that is your life. I just celebrated my sixty-third birthday, and when I think about some of my poor choices or consider the people who died without ever living—both young and old—or others who wasted lessons they could've learned, or still others who lost their way, I more clearly understand *amazing* and *incredible*!

Here's what I've learned:

1. *When I give my best, that will always be enough.* There will always be somebody smarter, more beautiful, and more accomplished at [fill in the blank]. I am inspired, not diminished, by their accomplishments. If I give 110 percent every time—win, lose, or draw—I have no regrets. Author Og Mandino says, "Always do your best—what you plant now, you will harvest later." And someone once said, "Nobody who ever gave her best regretted it."[8]

2. *Do the job right the first time because you can't recycle wasted time.* When I was a child, I learned, "If you can't find time to do it right, how will you find time to do it over?" That phrase haunts me because I reuse and recycle water bottles, cans, and newspapers—the usual—but if I waste time, I can blame it on traffic, failed alarm clocks, or too many meetings or activities. But the fact remains that it's *gone* and won't be back this side of glory.

   Each week we get 168 hours; remember to rest, play, delegate, appreciate, and celebrate so you can continue your journey to greatness.

3. *Invest.* In yourself, good health and nutrition, friends, others, and sound financial practices. When you invest in yourself, you get great dividends every day. And, since we are what we eat, get five to seven servings of fruits and vegetables daily or as often as you can. Drink more water and fewer sweetened beverages, and get moving. Treasure and make time for your friends. Mentor. Give, save, and spend—in that order. "You may be disappointed if you fail, but you will be doomed if you don't try" (Beverly Sills).

4. *Forgive.* Yourself, others, everybody who's done you wrong. Yes, today. You can decide later whether/how

---

8. This quote is attributed to George Halas.

much you want to forget, but continuing to hate is too heavy a burden for anyone to bear. I carried a Texas-sized box of hatred around for more than ten years before I realized that I was the only one suffering. Everyone else had moved on, but I was drowning from the cynicism, badmouthing, and hurt I was wallowing in and spewing onto anybody and everybody.

Trust me, letting go is/was hard for me, but I had to do it so I could move forward. There's still a scar from my woundedness, but I praise God that every year it fades a little more. Moving on may be difficult for you too, especially when you have been betrayed and violated by someone who was supposed to care for and protect you. If you've had your heart, body, and soul laid bare and dragged along the prairie like in the Westerns, healing takes time, but it does come. Begin by praying for them by name—prayer and hate cannot coexist in the same heart! Get some professional help. You have permission to grieve all that has been lost, but please *let it go*. You can't control the other person—don't worry about them. Do this for you.

Now that you mention it, I will/could/might/won't . . .

Use the space below to jot down some reflections after this reading.

_____

_____

_____

_____

_____

_____

11

What on Earth Is It and What Do You Do With It?

I have been packing boxes and bins feverishly, and here's what I know now: *too much stuff!* We all have entirely too much.

I know you're thinking, *What does she know about* my *stuff when she has so much of her own to sort through?* It's true, I don't know how much stuff you have swirling around you, *and* I have not opened your overstuffed hall closets or moved at least half of your furniture into the garage. I have, however, rolled my eyes after stepping on the twenty-fourth Barbie doll shoe that blended into the carpet and got caught between my toes. Maybe it was the shoes that helped me conclude that we, meaning you and I, have too much stuff, and we ought to do something about it. Use my handy checklist to get rid of some of your stuff before your next move. Not moving? Pretend! (And do it anyway.)

1. *You have something behind, on top of, underneath, or in every conceivable space*—corners, under the bed, behind the dining room buffet, in the living room couch cushions. What started out as a temporary storage space has now taken on permanency. *Solution:* Take one room at a time and look with a critical eye at everything. Anything you

don't absolutely loooove, take it to a consignment shop, donate it to Goodwill, sell it at a yard sale, share it with someone who would cherish it, or deposit it in the trash. *The upside:* fewer things to dust and a better view of the things you have left.

2. *Your cabinets and dresser drawers are so full, nothing else will fit. Solution:* Work on them while you're mindlessly watching *Family Feud* and *Rifleman* reruns. Throw away all the old underwear that would shame your mother if you were in an accident. Properly dispose of expired medicines, and next time, buy smaller containers to avoid waste. If you're saving empty medicine bottles for Vacation Bible School next year, suggest/select a container at church for collecting them. Clean out the drawers in the guest room, and move seasonal things to this under-utilized space to create more free room in your main areas. Buy some really cool containers/dividers to give your cabinets and drawers order. *The upside:* a place for everything and everything in its place—it's a beautiful thing!

3. *The things you never wear have taken over the closet. Solution:* 1/1/1. Every time you bring something in, something has to go out. If you haven't worn it in one year, it must meet the fate of stuff in suggestion number one of this list. Pay closer attention to your purchases, and if you answer *no* to any one of these four questions, flee the store immediately: (1) Can you wear it now? If it's too snug now, trust me, it won't stretch while hanging in the closet; (2) What else does this work with? Do an inventory before you go shopping so you know what you need. One way to stretch your wardrobe dollars is to buy good basics and refresh them annually with new accessories. Buy the best items you can afford on sale; (3) Is it stunning, and do you know you look good in it? Is it figure flattering? When you know you look good, you walk with and exude confidence no matter how hectic the day gets; (4) Is this a good color and style for you? Just because something's on sale doesn't make it a good deal. If it's the wrong color, size, or material, it won't serve you well. *The upside:* you and your closet look great!

Finally, my dears, stuff can be conquered once you define it and make a plan to get rid of it. Of course, if you're not packing and moving, you can always pretend you don't see it! Be blessed and keep shining! *Amen.*

Now that you mention it, I will/could/might/won't...

Use the space below to jot down some reflections after this reading.

_____

_____

_____

_____

_____

_____

_____

_____

12

Hello New Year, New Attitude, New Opportunities!

*B*lessings and best wishes this first month of the year as you celebrate, move forward, and soar! I love January because we get a chance to begin fresh, and I pray that's happening in every phase of your life. For me, it's a new home in a new city, new routines and challenges at work, home, and in the marketplace—Lordy, everything's new!

I have realized over the past six months that routine is what keeps me sane and on track. When chaos and change replace that, what comes next is often difficult and uncomfortable; but what I've learned has been very valuable. Here are four of my favorite lessons:

1. *Embrace change, roll with the flow, and grow strong.* Years ago I said, "Change belongs in your pocket," and I meant it. I know now that change doesn't have to be good or bad, it just *is* what it is. If you don't change, you die. We can change and grow incrementally, or we can be thrashed around like a sparrow in a hurricane. When we're lucky, we get to choose. Go ahead: dip your toe in, imagine where you can go and what you can be, and watch God do what only God loves to do—hold, protect, and love us unconditionally.

2. *Lighten your load.* I told my husband that he did not need twelve tackle boxes, sixty-five punch bowls, and ninety-nine fishing rods. If you have said items, the lesson is, you don't either! My husband collects "things," and they accumulate, so we always have more stuff than he realizes. The book *The Life-Changing Magic of Tidying Up: The Japanese Art of Decluttering and Organizing* by Marie Kondo encourages us to get rid of things that don't "spark joy." My friend Amanda had pictures of her efforts, and it was amazing how much stuff she didn't *need.* There is value in this exercise, whether you're moving or not. Most of us are attached to our stuff—either emotionally or in some significant way—so this may be easier said than done. But this year, work to declutter your mind, your home, and your life.

3. *Always make fun, friends, and fellowship time (FT).* The old adage, "All work and no play makes Cynthia Ann a dull girl," is true. If you're too busy to have lunch or spend quality time with your friends and loved ones, fix that. Your time is precious, so guard it carefully by prioritizing tasks and saying "no" to the "busyness" we get caught up in. When you do this, you can do things that make happy memories for later. Don't leave your FT to chance—put it on your calendar now so you know it's important. *And,* laughter is great medicine, so laugh until you cry at least seven times this week.

4. *When you can't find your shoes, ask for help.* We had lots of stuff at our old house (no surprise), and my moving method has always been like this: when moving day gets close, put the remaining "stuff" in a box, and label it as such. Somehow some of my labeled boxes of shoes destined for my closet got waylaid with the "stuff" boxes in the garage, and I haven't seen them since. Our new garage is much smaller and is now so full we can't even get a sheet of paper inside if we tried, so I have a couple pairs and that's it. I have surmised that the only way to find my shoes (and other missing items) is to ask my friends and loved ones to converge one Saturday

morning soon to clear out the garage boxes so my shoes can reappear and my car can go inside. So, lost shoes, heavy burdens, challenges, etc., are all the same: when we need help, ask! *Amen.*

Make this your best year ever!

Now that you mention it, I will/could/might/won't . . .
Use the space below to jot down some reflections after this reading.

13

Don't Even Think of Giving Up!

oday is *Ditch Your New Year's Resolutions Day,* and since I only made a few big ones, I can't decide which ones I want to leave on the cutting room floor. Seriously though, I suspect many of you made lofty ones too, so let's see where we are today and really get serious about moving forward tomorrow!

The problem with resolutions is that we need resolve to make them work. Saying you will get up earlier, leave home sooner, spend less, save more, lose weight, revamp the closets, yada, yada, yada, all sounded good at the time, but less than three weeks in, if we're not careful, our best-laid plans are headed out the door with the wrapping paper. Don't let them, and here's why:

1. *You're close to victory; don't give up yet.* Researchers tell us that it takes twenty-one days to permanently change habits—seventeen is not twenty-one. You're almost there! Refocus your energies, celebrate your successes, and analyze your missteps, but don't throw in the towel. In *31 Is Thirty-Wonderful: A Prayer and Reflection Journey/Journal for Triumphant Women,*[9] I asked busy women to take thirty-one minutes for thirty-one days to listen to/hear from God. Technically there's nothing magical about thirty-one days, but I discovered that the additional ten

---

9. *31 Is Thirty-Wonderful* is available on Kindle. Order it today from Amazon.com or www.touchedbygraceministry.com.

days of focused effort made sure new habits were fully formed, and you were truly on your way to triumphant. You're too close to turn back now.

2. *Don't get distracted by a technicality.* There was something so formal about the word *resolution* that I kept getting sidetracked. I started calling my plans "rungs" (like on a ladder), and I drew a ladder and labeled each rung with action steps that would get me to the top. Rungs, plans, resolutions, whatever—pick one and get going. The only way up is up!

3. *Make sure you have a timeline and strategic and specific steps— resolutions without timelines are just good intentions.* First, decide where/when you want to go, and then work backwards. Superstar Tina Turner told Oprah she plotted and planned her way to freedom. She knew how many concerts, albums, cities—you get the picture—it would take to reach her goals, and she stayed focused to get there. We must too—whether it's starting a business, retiring, or buying a new home or some cool wheels, begin with the end in mind (suggests best-selling author Stephen Covey). If you want to eat more fruits and vegetables, buy them instead of chips and Oreos (I had to block the Oreos from my cell because they kept texting me).

4. *Know your vulnerabilities.* If you have a difficult time saving money, stop shopping and put the money you would've spent in your dream account. If you need to lose weight, take a walk, drink more water, and make your lunch at home so you won't overspend or overeat! Be proactive and stay focused. *Amen.*

Now that you mention it, I will/could/might/won't . . .
Use the space below to jot down some reflections after this reading.

_____

_____

_____

14

I Do . . . Every Day

*B*eing married is fun! My husband, Roger, and I are best friends.[10] We adore each other, and yes, we finish each other's sentences, have the same thoughts at the same time—we call it ESP-N—and 99.1 percent of the time, we're on the same page. Please know I had to kiss a few frogs before God sent me this prince, but I thank God and my sister, Norma, for bringing us together.

Roger was one of Norma's friends, and she introduced us that first day I went job hunting at the University of Tennessee at Martin. He swears I took his breath away at first sight. I thought he was cute, but his ugly platform shoes with the laces on the side made me a tad suspicious. Norma had to go to class, so she trusted him to get me back to her dorm room. Instead he took me with him to class and wrote me mushy notes. The rest is history.

We've been together through undergraduate and graduate schools and the deaths of his mother, three of my four parents, and our remaining grandparents; we've had two hard-headed children who are now amazing parents themselves; we've had several jobs and bosses; we've been through nine moves and have travelled to all fifty states, six continents, and everything in between. Would we do it all over again? In a heartbeat!

---

10. Roger and Cynthia Bond Hopson are authors of the Amazon bestseller *I Do . . . Every Day: Wisdom for Newlyweds and Not So Newlyweds.*

As I praise God for our union and celebrate love and marriage this February, National Marriage Month, here are three things I *must* say:

1. *Those of us who believe in marriage must do more to support and advocate for it.* It seems popular to "play house," "live together," "shack up," or whatever they're calling it nowadays, but without vows, it's too easy to walk away when things don't go well. Marriage ought to be a partnership—rarely will it be 50/50, but it's a commitment, not math.

2. *Marriage takes constant attention.* If you have a job and you do just enough to get by, you don't get raises or promotions like you would if you gave it 110 percent. Marriage is the same way. You *must* pay attention to, trust, and respect your relationship. Go on dates, make time for love and intimacy, and work at making your home a refuge rather than another war zone.

3. *Kindness always matters.* Harsh words, once spoken, can't be softened or taken back, no matter how many times you say you're sorry. Roger and I encourage, cajole, inspire, support, defend, and stretch each other, but we know confusion lurks when we don't talk. Certainly we *must* listen, but we *must* be sensitive to things that are unspoken too. Roger and I fully understand that God blessed us with each other—may you, too, be blessed in your love and marriage. Stay in love with God and each other. *Amen.*

Now that you mention it, I will/could/might/won't . . .

Use the space below to jot down some reflections after this reading.

_____

_____

_____

_____

_____

15

It's Spring—
Let's Celebrate!

I love spending snow days stuck inside, watching *Gunsmoke*, *The Virginian*, *The Big Valley*, and *Bonanza* more than anybody I know, but if there's a choice between snowmen or daffodils and robins, it's absolutely a no-brainer! I love everything about spring—the hope that seems to spring forth like the tulips in the morning dew and the gorgeous flowers and trees that bud and bloom as a gentle reminder that Easter is coming soon! *Everything* shouts, *Glory, hallelujah!*

Since it's spring, we have to have an official "Spring To-Do List":

1. *Start with your closet.* Think three—if you haven't worn it in three years, do one of three things with it: (1) consign it, (2) donate it, or (3) include it in the yard sale you should be planning! Lighten your load and start fresh.

2. *Evaluate the shoes.* Do you have to lie down to put them on? If so, give them a proper burial and replace them. If they look like you got them from Chris (also known as Christopher Columbus) after he got them from Izzie (also known as Queen Isabella of Spain, in 1492), send them to a new world. Remember, if they hurt your feet the last time you wore them, nothing has changed. When in doubt, see number one above.

3. *Spruce up your yard/porch/patio, and create an official contemplation spot* where you go after a long, hard, ugly day, or where you leave the phone inside and admire the morning and the sunrise and listen to your breathing while you and God plan your day.

4. *Celebrate National Women's History Month* and donate to a cause that is dear to your heart in memory or honor of the phenomenal women who invested in and shaped you. Send a note, call, or stop by to see your heroines and make their day. Bask in where God has brought you from and where you are today—*celebrate you and God*, for heaven's sake!

5. *Do more of what makes you happy and less of what doesn't!* Oh, if you don't have allergies, pick up a bunch of fresh flowers for your kitchen counter—they'll brighten your day and your mood. *Need I say more?*

6. *This week, be kind on purpose*—it's like taking the road less traveled. It will make all the difference. "We rise by lifting others" (Robert G. Ingersoll).

7. *Let whatever you do today be enough!* I read this on a plaque yesterday and it spoke directly to me. Think about it. We want more, try to do more, accomplish more, when in actuality, we are already *all that*—hot chocolate chip cookies and chilled Sprite. *You are absolutely enough! Amen.*

Happy spring, and happy Women's History Month!

Now that you mention it, I will/could/might/won't ...
Use the space below to jot down some reflections after this reading.

_____

_____

_____

_____

_____

16

You Is Beautiful

*I*n the 2011 movie *The Help,* Aibileen Clark kept repeating to her young charge: "You is beautiful, you is smart, and you is important."[11] Today these nine words are for you too if you've been sexually abused, molested, raped, or violated.

April is National Sexual Abuse Awareness Month, and this month I want you to be fully aware so you can do your part to stop, report, help to restore, forgive, handle the business—whatever the case may be.

> ❧ *Be aware of the statistics.* Every two minutes another American is sexually assaulted.[12] Multiply that by the number of conflict-torn countries where rape is often used as an instrument of war and destruction, and you begin to see what our challenges are. While women are the usual victims, the number of men who are sexually assaulted continues to grow. Children and women worldwide being sold into slavery, pornography, and sex trafficking require more weeks' worth of discussion.

> ❧ *Be aware of the impact.* It is a scar that never fully heals. Sixty percent of sexual assaults are not reported to police, and 97 percent of rapists never spend a day in jail.[13] In most cases the offenders are not strangers.

> ❧ *Be aware of your role* in healing, helping, preventing, and reporting. If you see it, say something. If you suspect it, investigate. If you are afraid you will become an abuser,

---

11. *The Help,* based on the book by Kathryn Stockett, 2011, Dreamworks Films.
12. www.rainn.org/statistics
13. Ibid.

get help. If you've been a victim, seek counseling to rebuild trust and to put your life back together—to forgive and move forward.

❧ *Discuss "touch" with your children.* Show them what is "good" and "inappropriate" touch, and tell them how to react/respond to both. If your child has the courage to tell you something is amiss, listen.

❧ *Today, read and learn* as much as you can about this often-invisible problem so you can become an advocate for the innocents and part of the healing process for those you love and care about. The statistics are sad and staggering, yet there is hope and restoration. We were created by a loving God who wants us to live triumphantly and enjoy our lives, our bodies, and our choices.

On Easter you received the right to again be beautiful, important, and smart, no matter what your past looks like. Claim it! Live into it! Build on it! Speaking beauty, truth, and life into your dailiness is a great beginning! Bishop T. D. Jakes reminds us, "We need to invest in our own deliverance." And so we must, and awareness is the first step. What you do next is up to you. *Amen.*

Now that you mention it, I will/could/might/won't . . .

Use the space below to jot down some reflections after this reading.

_____

_____

_____

_____

_____

_____

17

The Least We Can Do Is Make Our Mom Proud

My mother, Mrs. Alvis Marie Jones Bond, doesn't cry when she's happy or gush over things like I do. Trust me, I cry at mushy notes, sappy movies, sweet songs on the radio—whatever strikes me that day. And yes, when she says, "that was nice," or "I really enjoyed it"—whatever *it* was, I know to take that and rejoice because it's probably not going to get any mushier than that.

I never heard her brag on us like my dad did; give him five minutes and he could run down the current status and accomplishments of eight young'uns in a heartbeat. But I know she must've done her share, because whenever I would visit her school before she retired as a teacher's aide, I'd have to answer, "No, I'm not the one who got a promotion at FedEx; no I'm not the one who just moved to California [etc.]. Yes, I'm the one who did [so and so]."

My mother would just smile as I'd try to explain which of my highly accomplished siblings I wasn't. Somehow she has made all four of the sons-in-law believe they're her favorites, and they fight over who gets the most special treatment and which one she likes best. She just laughs and reminds them they're all like her sons. The daughters-in-law adore her as well.

She is as smart as she is beautiful, witty, and wise, and every day she is more precious than the day before. I laugh often about how she didn't work outside our home when we were little, but when she did get a job, it was at our school. She was *way* too handy for teachers who didn't mind doing serious discipline. She went to school when we went and came back when we came back. Homemade biscuits were always a part of our hot breakfasts, and there wasn't a latchkey kid to be found.

She was at the top of her class in high school and was headed to college before she met and fell in love with our dad, her husband of fifty-one years. So many jobs and careers she would've been highly qualified for, but she chose to put her family first. I will always be grateful for her sacrifice. Once she introduced me for an event, and she spoke about the amazing woman I'd become and how proud she was of me—all the things I would've wanted to hear. Of course I was a blubbering mess by the time she finished, but she never broke a sweat. For me, making her proud ranked right on up there with winning an Oscar, the Pulitzer, *and* the Nobel Prize for literature!

My beautiful mother-in-law was equally amazing. She'd proudly introduce me: "This is my daughter—she's a doctor!" Widowed at thirty-three with nine children, she stood strong and courageously and showed the world what pride, dignity, and true grit looked like. She surely could have been the model for Maya Angelou's now infamous *Phenomenal Woman*. Her legacy of love, empowerment, and perseverance are the things legends are made of.

As Mother's Day approaches, think about all the *moms* (Big Mama, Madea, GG, Auntie, your best friend's mom, the next-door neighbor, your big sister, your dad—all of the MamaNems, as comedian Jonathan Slocumb calls them) who have poured the best of themselves into you. Call or send some flowers, a note, a gift card, something—to say thanks for investing in who you've become. If your mom is no longer alive, pay it forward and do a deed that would make her smile. Oh, be blessed and keep making her proud.

Oh, by the way . . . here's another word of appreciation to our mothers, other mothers, grandmothers, aunts, sisters, and Damas (Dads who had to be mamas too):

We really do see you, though there is no way we can fully understand and appreciate the enormity and impact of the gift you have given us—life, direction, courage, wisdom, good sense, strength, sometimes a good cussing when our heads were hard. But this Mother's Day, it is important to say, *We see you.* We love you, we appreciate everything about you, and we are thankful to and for you. Thankful that you took time to love, hug, encourage, and be here, there, and seemingly everywhere. And not just *thank you* this day, you beautiful, dynamic, and sophisticated creation of an awesome God, but for all you've done in the days past and the ones to come. We salute you this day.

Now that you mention it, I will/could/might/won't . . .

Use the space below to jot down some reflections after this reading.

18

Call Me Mater!

*M*ater—like *tomato* without the *ta!*"

I'm loving that it's officially summer, and if homegrown tomatoes aren't careful, by October they'll be an endangered species. I loved tomatoes long before the movie *Cars* made this hilarious line famous, and when I see little ones, big ones, and whatever comes in between, I'm always tempted to grab one, rub it on my pant leg, and chomp on it as the juice runs down my chin.

The only things more wonderful than homegrown tomatoes might possibly be fresh green beans, tiny new potatoes, sweet corn, okra, yummy peaches and strawberries (in a pie or not), or juicy watermelon! June is Fruit and Veggies Month, and I think we ought to *eat* like we know it!

If the adage, "We are what we eat," is true, and I believe it is, consider what we could avoid if we paid more attention to what we ate. Probably our risks for hypertension, stroke, cardiovascular and dental-related ailments, diabetes, and obesity would diminish. For every sweet soda, giant candy bar, fried chicken leg, and couch potato moment we enjoy, the chance of getting into that eensie weensie yellow polka dot bikini fades like the morning dew. My friends, *we can choose different outcomes!* Here's how:

> ✧ *Exercise* at least three times a week for at least thirty minutes—every day would be ideal, but the key here is consistency. Get off your "blessed assurance," as Bishop Bill McAlilly puts it, and shake your shimmy during commercials and park at the far end of the parking lot instead of taking the front-door spot. Don't

let your doctor keep prescribing more drugs—control any new concerns with diet and exercise, if possible. For every dollar I give Walgreens, I have fewer for Stein Mart and Macy's. I choose the Mart and Macy's.

❧ *Think* before you eat. Are you hungry, or is it simply time to eat? Chew more slowly, and when you're full, stop eating! As a child I had to eat everything on my plate, and I was sure if I didn't, I would be turned into a pumpkin. It ain't necessarily so! Now I use three saucers at the buffet—including dessert. This controls portions and keeps me from overeating. An old weight-loss commercial advocated leaving a few bites on your plate every meal. Try it.

❧ *Have* at least eight glasses of water and seven servings of fruits and vegetables daily. This morning I captured the cold water (on the way to hot) from the faucet in a half gallon cup. I'm drinking it as my earth-friendly opportunity. It would've been wasted otherwise. Veggies and water improve your skin and body functions, and you'll look and feel better.

❧ *Stop* dieting. Many of us have lost and gained the same fifteen pounds on some newfangled plan that didn't require healthy eating and exercise. After somebody made millions, we realized the endorsements were fake, and we were still overweight. Remember, you heard it here first—there's no substitute for healthy eating and exercise.

Let's vow to make every month Fruit and Veggies Month, and whether they're calling us 'Mater or 'Tater, please step right up and answer!

Now that you mention it, I will/could/might/won't . . .

Use the space below to jot down some reflections after this reading.

_____

_____

_____

19

Here's a Cheer for Great Dads!

*W*hen Miss Olivia Michelle Burgess arrived at 6 pounds, 5 ounces, her father (and my nephew), Wesley Everett Burgess, announced her triumphant arrival and held her proudly so her whole generation could admire her and bask in his delight. Olivia is his firstborn, and her appearance just in time for Father's Day was perfect, thanks to her beautiful mom, Dannielle.

As we celebrate Father's Day this year, I remember the lessons, laughter, and love I received from my own amazing and precious father, John. This year I'd like to share 10½ of my favorite Big John lessons:

1. If you're going to get in trouble, do it on your own and not because you were following the crowd.

2. If you will always remember to *think*, you can avoid a whole bunch of trouble.

3. Have your own money so you won't have to stand around looking stupid.

4. If a train leaves the station and stays on track, it *will* reach its destination.

5. Words matter. Think long and hard about what you say so you won't have to eat your words later. Learn all you can.

6. Just because you can do a thing doesn't mean you should. It may not be wrong, but it may not be expedient at this time.

7. Your word is your bond. If you say you'll do a thing, be found trying to get it done.

8. Treat others the way you want to be treated. You're no better than anybody else, but you're as good as anybody else.

9. Be careful with your reputation because "I was a little boy once, and I know what little boys do." (My dad was over six feet tall with hands the size of baseball gloves—I couldn't imagine there was ever a time when he was a little boy, but he sure was right about those little nasty boys and their agendas!)

10. Laughter really is the best medicine! He loved to laugh, and when he did, it made me laugh too.

10½. You can trust God with *anything* and *everything* that concerns you.

My father, John A. Bond Jr., died September 4, 2004, and there are very few days when I don't remember something he said or get some other gentle reminder of him. I can remember these wonderful lessons because he lived them every day. My precious memories also include my other dad, my great-uncle Carey, who had the most beautiful brown eyes—they danced when he laughed, which was often. He gave everybody some wacky nickname and loved to "carry on foolishness," as he called it. He was compassionate and kind and taught me to see the beauty and humanity in others.

I praise God for my husband, Roger, who is cut from the same cloth as my two heroes and is a great father and an over-the-top Poppy to our four grandchildren and Avery, our great-grandson. A special salute and blessing to my son, Marcos, my wonderful brothers—the ones I got the easy way and the ones I got by law, my nephews, and my friends who get up every day and provide guidance, love, honor, and care for their families. Let us continue to pray for our neighbors who are separated from their children as they work to offer a better life for their generations to come. *Amen.*

Now that you mention it, I will/could/might/won't . . .
Use the space below to jot down some reflections after this reading.

_____

_____

_____

_____

_____

_____

_____

_____

_____

20

Use Your Own Stuff

One of my favorite remembrances from childhood involves my great-aunt/mother Emma's cedar chest. This beautiful piece of furniture didn't reach the top of the mattress, but it lived at the foot of the bed. It was made from cedar, hence its name, and wasn't quite as wide as the bed. Anyway, it had a nice tray inside and contained all her *really* nice things. You know, the beautiful sheets, towels, sweaters—stuff that was too nice to use every day. It was strictly reserved for "company," though I never saw it brought out for use by the four million visitors (or so it seemed) who frequented our home.

About twice a year on a quiet night, she and I would pull up our chairs and open it up. We'd *ooh* and *aww* over the beautiful things inside, take them out, and refold them and close it until next time. One day, about three years before her death, I was visiting and the facecloths were almost threadbare. Of course I knew she had some better ones, so I asked why she wasn't using some of those gorgeous ones from the cedar chest. She admitted that she hated to use them because they were so pretty or weren't sturdy enough for daily use.

I assured her she was caring a lot more about those things than anyone else would. I even promised her that after she was gone, I was going to use them every day. I encouraged her to go to that darned chest, get those gorgeous things that were probably dry-rotted by now, and enjoy them. They had been gifts to her, so I said she should be the one to feel their plushness while wallowing on those expensive thread counts. I said, "Don't leave them for some other big-headed woman to enjoy!" (The saga of the big-headed woman is a story for another day, but suffice it to say, that was all the convincing she needed!)

So my dears, wear that fancy dress, get those beautiful dishes and those nice heavy forks out, and enjoy them. Heck, it doesn't matter if you're only eating a peanut butter and jelly sandwich—trust me, because of the beauty of your "things," it'll be like filet mignon! When you're gone, your fancy towels will be left behind for somebody to wash the car with, or your Waterford crystal may be on the patio for the dog's water or come to some other similar fate. *Use and enjoy your own stuff!* This Sunday, treat your family like company, and refuse to treat strangers better than the ones you love.

Enjoy *all* the beauty around you. Start with yourself, your heart, and your spirit. Then move on, admiring the color purple, spider webs in the morning dew, sunrises, and sunsets—everything. Oh, and give thanks for the journey!

Now that you mention it, I will/could/might/won't . . .

Use the space below to jot down some reflections after this reading.

_____

_____

_____

_____

_____

_____

_____

21

My Daddies Put the Happy in Father's Day

I'm just about the happiest woman in the whole world, and here's why. I had two amazing daddies who adored me, were beautiful inside and out, and helped make me the woman I am today. Very few days pass without them or their lessons coming to mind. They were gentle but strong, confident but humble, kind, great providers, heart from head to foot, and they lived out their faith. I have never been hungry or had to wonder where my next meal or provisions would come from. Please know, I'm not bragging; I'm simply praising God for creating these heroes and putting them in my life.

Carey Bowles, my great-uncle who helped raise me, had a third-grade education but could out-calculate me in his head any day. He taught me to always pay attention, because "everything you need to know won't be in a book." He loved his siblings and friends unconditionally. He and his best friend, Davis "Buster/Farmer" Brown, often played checkers and would argue and fuss, so my great-aunt threatened to send Mr. Buster home!

My dad-dad, John A. "Big John" Bond, was bigger than life. My sister and I were laughing last month when one of my brothers had to give Dad's "I was a little boy once" talk with his daughter. He was always bigger than life, so we couldn't imagine him ever being little or having a clue about what boys do. He and my mother had great expectations for us, and the eight of us worked to make them proud. He loved words and said he could work with anyone—as long as he was the boss!

Research shows that women who have great fathers often try to find their fathers in the men they marry. It's true. My husband is a magical combination of both of them. Today much of what we hear about fatherhood is negative, but today's fathers can be great too—and here's how we can help:

- ✺ Don't believe the hype: *Women can teach boys how to be men,* but they shouldn't have to do it by themselves. It does take a village, and the responsible, positive male villagers, no matter their age, must invest in these boys, mentor and coach them, and model good behavior for them.

- ✺ Remind your sons, grandsons, brothers, etc., to cultivate and nurture the seeds they plant. Don't even fix your mouth to say, "I'm glad I don't have girls," because every time a young woman has an unplanned pregnancy, like the old Shake 'n Bake commercial for baked chicken, somebody helped! (Do the paternity tests early if you're unsure!) Providing for children's physical needs is certainly important, but making certain children feel wanted, safe, and cared for ranks right there at the top too. We must define the difference between the quantity and the quality of time—it's critical to be *there* when you're *there.*

- ✺ Encourage and praise the good traits you see in the fathers you know. They may just be doing what they're supposed to do, but we all like praise, especially when it's for something this important. Have events to provide parenting advice, resources, or respite for those who are struggling or juggling work/life balance issues. Teach the lessons you've learned without being preachy.

Now that you mention it, I will/could/might/won't . . .
Use the space below to jot down some reflections after this reading.

_____

_____

_____

_____

_____

_____

_____

_____

_____

22

Life Is Like Ice Cream

*J*uly is National Ice Cream Month, and I intend to celebrate often and enthusiastically! The somebody who suggested this wonderful celebration should receive special commendation for this delicious excuse to indulge!

My earliest ice cream remembrances are around a hand-cranked freezer, anticipating its yummy contents. If ice cream is ever offered, I take it. And no matter how it's packaged—straight from the homemade canister, on a stick, in a cup/bowl with a wooden stick, in a waffle cone—I'm for it.

I was pondering the deep meanings of life this week, and I have concluded that ice cream is a lot like life. Hear me out:

1. Like ice cream, life offers lots of choices. My father worked at an ice cream factory when I was growing up, so we were always pretty popular in our community. He'd bring new flavors for us to test, so when Baskin-Robbins came along with thirty-one flavors, I didn't get the fascination because we'd always had thirty-one or more. There's chocolate and mint, chocolate and peanut butter, marshmallows, nuts, all of the above, or just chocolate. Life is like that. You can be adventurous, or you can stay in your comfort zone, never trying new foods, places, or things. You can have butter pecan or black walnut, and if you can't decide, you can sample until you find something

you like. There are no wrong answers—maybe a little bellyaching if you overindulge—but *you* get to choose.

2. If left unattended, ice cream becomes a soggy, runny mess. Need I say more? If you've ever left ice cream uncovered in the freezer or on the cabinet, in a very short while, it's melted and yucky. Trust me, our lives are the same way. If we're not careful about diet, exercise, enrichment, and relationships, before long we're in shambles. Life, like ice cream, takes special handling, attention to detail, and careful consumption. If you've ever eaten ice cream too fast and gotten what's called "brain freeze," where your whole head throbs, life is definitely that way. Everything has a time, a reason, and a season.

3. Beware of the shiny objects on aisle three. There are premium brands, store brands, and those in between. The more expensive brands tout their purity, all-natural ingredients, and superior taste in fancy packaging. Store brands may taste as good and cost less but get overlooked because their presentation doesn't reach out and grab us. Think about all the things in life we overlook, devalue, and/or miss simply because they aren't flashy, fast, and "hip." Many athletes/entertainers learn the hard way that the people who knew and loved them before they became rich and famous will usually be the ones who're still there when the applause and bright lights are gone. They "stick and stay," as my great-grandmother called it, tell us the truth whether we want to hear it or not, and gently remind us what's important.

4. Finally, life, like ice cream, is meant to be enjoyed—savored. Certainly you can derive pleasure from me ranting and raving about the finer points of ice cream sandwiches, waffle cones, and all the wonderful flavors I find at my favorite parlors, but nothing compares to eating your own! Trying a new flavor or adventure doesn't mean you're disloyal to vanilla and chocolate.

But just for this month, add chocolate chips, or Oreos, something, and experience every bite—even let a little run down your chin and fingers—and embrace both ice cream and life in a whole new way.

Now that you mention it, I will/could/might/won't …

Use the space below to jot down some reflections after this reading.

_____

_____

_____

_____

_____

_____

_____

_____

23

Kindness Matters

Here's what I know for sure this week: (1) being kind is almost as important as breathing; (2) even the smallest acts of kindness are remembered; (3) kindness really matters.

Certainly I know these things every day of the year, but this is National Be Kind to Humankind Week, and it's important that we be kinder than usual. I suspect if we do it on purpose this week, it might become part of our routine.

As legend would have it, Canadian Lorraine Jara started this weeklong celebration twenty-eight years ago to promote kindness after she read a mean-spirited article. I am grateful she's gently reminding us to be more civil and thoughtful in our actions and reactions. Think about it: most of the folks we know are nice and helpful, and if we take time to build relationships with the ones who aren't, we soon discover that deep down we all want the same things—to be affirmed, admired, and included.

There was a woman at our church who was so mean she'd give snakes a bad name! As I got to know her though, I discovered that when life gave her lemons, she sucked until there was no juice left for lemonade or lemon meringue pie (my preferred uses). She didn't respond to kindness at first, but over the years, she became a trusted friend and mentor. I almost missed this blessing because her baaaad attitude sent me in the opposite direction!

Here's your to-do list for this week:

- Whatever makes your day—having lunch with a friend, receiving flowers or a sweet card, or getting those emails that distract you from your work and make you giggle—do that for someone else.

- Re-record your voicemail message, and this time smile or share a happy thought—even if it's a telemarketer, you'll brighten their day.

- Yield to the driver who is trying to get out of a parking lot or who needs to get over. Pray for the person who cuts you off in traffic, and instead of yelling profanities, wave and say, "God bless you."

- Practice giving every person you meet a smile or affirmation. Don't make up stuff, but find something to admire and compliment. And this week especially, accept all compliments graciously and with a simple "thank you."

- Do anonymous and random acts every Monday in September and October. Oh, and keep shining!

Now that you mention it, I will/could/might/won't . . .

Use the space below to jot down some reflections after this reading.

_____

_____

_____

_____

_____

_____

_____

24

Happy "Be Kind to Humankind" Week!

This week is our perfect opportunity to spread some kindness, peace, joy, love, and civility, and show the world what we're made of. Yes, I'm asking you to add one more thing to your to-do list this week—trust me, if you choose even one thing off the list below, it will tickle God's heart.

To-Do List for Be Kind to Humankind Week

1. *Shut up and listen.* I was listening to National Public Radio today, and a segment about a suicide hotline volunteer touched me immensely. The speaker said the big *shut up and listen* sign posted on the wall of the prevention center was a gentle reminder of the critical importance of listening. Not to fix things, not to offer solutions, not to pass judgment—just to listen and be comfortable with silence. Sometimes we need silence to gather our thoughts and gently decipher what we're trying to say. Let's pause, be active listeners, and pay attention to body language and key words so we hear what is, as well as what isn't, being said.

2. *Be intentional.* Some folks just have to whine and complain, and they're not satisfied until we are miserable too. They make being kind difficult, but be kind anyway. The hurt

that's manifesting itself in this cruel, hard exterior is a protective shell to avoid further hurt. The folks who deserve kindness the least are the ones who need it most. When in doubt, do #1.

3. *Follow your first mind.* My dear Uncle Carey always said, "My first mind told me . . ." and I always wondered how many minds he had. But as I got older, I understood. Your first thought is usually right and your most valuable—follow that one. If a visit with Aunt Lucy comes to mind, go now and see her for a hug and some caramel cake. If a thought or a person keeps coming to mind, say a prayer if you can't follow up, but don't put important things off for tomorrow.

4. *If it touched your heart, do it for others.* When grief or tragedy strikes, knowing what to do is often difficult. Here's what not to do: Don't fix your mouth to say, "If you need me, call me." Usually in these situations, the somebody you said that to is in such a place, they haven't a clue what they need. Think about what would be helpful if your whole world were upside down. When there's a death, I try to gather paper products—paper towels, tissue, napkins, foil, garbage bags, plates, cups, plasticware (stuff you need but don't think about or have enough of for the hordes that come)—and take them the first day. I also take postage stamps and give them to someone who will know where they are when it's time to write thank you notes.

5. *Make today count: volunteer.* Whether it's spending time at the food pantry or the Humane Society, reading to someone whose eyesight has failed, delivering Meals on Wheels—you decide; helping others is the perfect pick-me-up, and that smile you get lasts all day! If you are too busy to spare an hour or two a month, my dears, you are too busy.

6. *Get to know one of your neighbors or church members.* We've gotten so busy and churches are so large that we come and go without a clue who lives next door or who's next

to us on the pew. Aim to get to know at least one new person every week in September.

7. *Make someone's day.* Send a mushy note or flowers today, and remember, kindness matters!

Now that you mention it, I will/could/might/won't . . .

Use the space below to jot down some reflections after this reading.

_____

_____

_____

_____

_____

_____

_____

_____

_____

25

Grand Is the Perfect Word . . . As in Grandchildren

*I*f heaven is any more wonderful than grandchildren, I don't think I can stand it! I am Kiera, Terrell, Maya, and Morgan's Grandmama, and GiGi and Avery's 2G (great-grandmother), so if I die right now, I've already experienced heaven. As Grandparents Day approaches, I gotta tell you, I'm loving every minute of it!

My husband, Roger, and I often laugh about how, before our grandchildren came, he swore he wasn't going to be like all these other grandparents with the mile-high brag books and the endless stories about cute grandchildren. He doesn't have their first pictures, but give him .31 seconds, and he'll be ranting and raving like every other grandparent.

I can't explain why having grandchildren is so much fun, but with two little ones—Morgan and Maya are eleven and twelve—and two big ones—Terrell just graduated from college and Kiera is twenty-seven—we just know they are. Yes, it has to do with being able to send them home when you've stepped on one too many Barbie shoes or tried to bathe but the Legos have first dibs, but maybe we see an opportunity to fix whatever we weren't sure about the first time. Perhaps we're in a different place and phase in our lives, and we know what really matters. Either way, here are my hopes and dreams for all of us Meemaws, PaPaws, Grans, Grannies, and wannabes:

- *If you don't have any grandchildren of your own, stop your whining and borrow some.* Too many children need someone to dote on them and make them the star of the show. Unfortunately some grandparents have to go another round with child rearing because drugs, death, poverty, and destruction have decimated our families and communities. Single parents are struggling to keep food on the table and may not have time to hug, encourage, and love on their little people. Look around you and lend a hand, especially if you're lamenting how you don't have any grandbabies and may not get any.

- *Be on the same page with Mom and Dad.* OK, I admit my grandchildren get away with stuff my children never did, but we try to listen and support rather than do our thing and let our children do theirs. That is unhelpful. My job is to love and spoil them, and I'm doing my very best to be as awesome as my four grandparents were. It was always a treat to visit them, and while they were different from my parents, we always had to mind our manners, not be attitudinal, and do what they asked. Nothing about that changed.

- *Finally, volunteer at your local elementary school, daycare, or neonatal unit.* Yes, they run a background check to protect you and the children, but volunteering to rock hospital-bound babies or to hug and encourage the children is a wonderful investment in a child's life and into making a more just, peaceful, and civil world. Grandparents Day comes the second Sunday in September—love from grandchildren comes every day!

Now that you mention it, I will/could/might/won't …
Use the space below to jot down some reflections after this reading.

_____

_____

_____

_____

_____

_____

_____

_____

_____

26

Take Care of the "Girls" All Year

October is Breast Cancer Awareness Month, and in my humble opinion, every month ought to be breast health month! Your body is such an amazing instrument. When it speaks—like the old E. F. Hutton commercials[14] used to say—you should listen. The conversation around when/whether to get a mammogram continues to swirl around us, yet the fact remains that far too many of us are dying because we don't pay attention to self-exams and small or subtle changes that hint something may be awry. We know our bodies better than anyone else, and with the "girls," our beautiful breasts, they aren't just body parts—they feed our babies, bring us pleasure and confidence, and a whole host of things. *We must take care of them and ourselves!*

I once had a doctor who didn't listen—she simply wanted yes or no answers and told me so in no uncertain terms. I was having womanly-part troubles, and I had not taken my medicine correctly. I was feeling lousy, and as I kept trying to figure out why, I actually read that little insert that's attached to your medicine—you know, the one we usually ignore. Anyway, at about three that morning, I realized that my sore legs and

---

14. E. F. Hutton & Co. was an American stock brokerage firm founded in 1904 by Edward Francis Hutton and his brother, Franklyn Laws Hutton. A series of commercials during the 1980s showed the namesake's enormous influence in a scene that portrayed how everyone stopped what they were doing to hear what he had to say. The line bragged, "When E. F. Hutton speaks, people listen."

racing heartbeat were "side effects" that had developed. If there were ten things that could go wrong, I had 9.5 of them!

I could hardly wait until morning to call and get further instruction. The nurse said I needed to see my primary care physician as soon as possible. My primary care physician was new, and I was all excited about bonding with her and developing a relationship for my care. I knew explaining what was going on would be important because every indicator said I was dying, had heebie-jeebies, or a million other horrible diseases! Her first questions frustrated both of us. She finally cut me off in the middle of an explanation with, "Just yes or no please." I was devastated and left there feeling about the size of a Wizard of Oz munchkin, but here's what I learned:

> *A doctor who won't/ doesn't listen doesn't deserve my trust, time, or money.* My "real" doctor took one look at me that Thursday and said, "Sit down and tell me what's going on with you." Thirty minutes and thirty years later, she rose, wrote me a prescription for Iyanla VanZant's *Value in the Valley*, and sent me on my way. No drugs, just this book that gently reminded me it was OK to be where I was. I just needed someone to listen.

> *Pain is information, and prevention is the best cure.* This month, schedule your mammogram, but get your other annual and periodic exams too—pap smear, eyes, feet, colon—anything you love and that contributes to your quality of life. Most diseases are preventable and treatable with early detection.

> *Your body is highly sophisticated,* so don't even try to diagnose yourself on the internet! Like new cars and cell phones, your body has tons of intricate bells and whistles you can't entrust to folks who work under a shade tree with two screwdrivers and a wrench. I swear, with mammograms they're just checking to make sure the "girls" are hooked on good; but seriously, a little discomfort now is a pretty small tradeoff for what could happen if you ignore this simple procedure.

> *There are several sites that offer free mammograms.* Google "free mammograms" for a local site. Make it a Girls

Day Out for you, your friends, your mom, sisters, aunts—fill in the blank. Have lunch, go to the local beauty school for a facial, manicure, and pedicure—so you'll know that the people you love are OK. Better yet, for your birthday this year, sponsor this blessing for a woman at a homeless shelter or someone who might forego this exam because she can't afford it.

❧ *If you take care of yourself first, everything else falls into place.* It's fine if you take care of other folks—bask in the knowledge that you are a selfless soul—but be clear that putting self-care at the bottom of your to-do list does not serve you well. You are the heart of your family, and we'll still be looking for you to get up from your sick bed and do whatever it is you always do whether you're tired, overworked, or overrun. Try saying "no" once in a while. *No* is a complete sentence, and you won't be turned into a pumpkin if/when you confidently use it as a self-care mechanism. Like the Nike commercial says, "Just do it," and briskly walk away before the guilt patrol descends. And, for those who can't walk fast: write the word *something* on your calendar at least three days this month, then you simply reply, "I'm sorry I can't, I already have something on my calendar."

Like flight attendants tell you in the life-saving instructions before takeoff: "Put your mask on first." My dears, you are amazing, precious, and beautiful! Take care of the "girls" and the rest of you so we can spread our wings and soar together!

Now that you mention it, I will/could/might/won't . . .

Use the space below to jot down some reflections after this reading.

_____

_____

_____

_____

_____

27

Aim for Stunning

A s a child growing up in rural Tennessee, I loved watching television on Saturday evening to see one of my favorites, *The Porter Wagoner Show.* The show opened with Mr. Wagoner making his way through the studio with his fancy clothes as he prepared to sing and welcome his guests. His stunning jacket and slacks had these rhinestone wagon wheels on them, and he was always immaculate—unlike many of the entertainers today who look like they get their clothes from the hamper before they perform. A handsome man with beautiful hair and cool clothes—he was mighty impressive.

Mr. Wagoner, in an interview a few years before he died, said something that inspires me still. He grew up poor and said that when he became successful, he understood how privileged he was that audiences would sacrifice their hard-earned money to come to his concerts. He said he always wanted to look his best so he could give his best and be at his best, because his fans deserved that.

I agree wholeheartedly, and every time I leave home, whether for work, church, speaking, singing, or just plain ol' being, I aim for stunning and positive because I, too, am privileged to have this opportunity. Growing up, I never dreamed I'd escape the endless rows of cotton or leave the dusty country roads, but praise God, I did. (And though I never thought I'd say it, I have lamented how simple life was in the cotton fields!)

Today though, I fully understand that somebody paid a hefty price so I could follow my dreams—heck, so I could even have a dream! Perhaps it was my great-grandmother who lived in somebody else's home and scrubbed floors, or maybe it was my parents who were both very smart but had to forego college because with eight of us, they couldn't afford to go. Maybe it was Miss Georgia, the University of Memphis custodian who saw me wandering in the Meeman Journalism Building on my first day. She said, "Baby, I didn't get to go to college, and here you are teaching here. I'm just so proud." Her encouragement helped me become the department's first tenured African American associate professor. I am certain *The Women of Haywood*,[15] whose powerful and triumphant lives kept me focused when the going got tough, paid part of that price too.

Today we must remember that someone's sacrifice has opened every door we've entered. Yes, you are beautiful and smart, but you didn't get/couldn't have gotten where you are without somebody helping you along the way. I love a quote credited to *Roots* author Alex Haley that says, "If you see a turtle on top of a fencepost, you know he had some help." Honor that with humility and compassion.

Lift as you climb, and keep the door open—kick in a few, and lend a hand, heart, or a word of encouragement. Whether the pants have rhinestones like Mr. Wagoner's or not, always do your best. For every show, no matter how much the tickets cost. *Amen.*

Now that you mention it, I will/could/might/won't . . .

Use the space below to jot down some reflections after this reading.

---

15. *The Women of Haywood: Their Lives, Our Legacy*, is a collection of oral histories of four professional African American women in Haywood County, TN. It is available on Kindle.

28

We Must Talk about Domestic Abuse

My husband, Roger, and I often teased that he would never hit me because my father, Big John, was more than six feet tall, had hands like baseball gloves, and was a no-nonsense kind of guy. In reality, he was a gentle giant who died fourteen years ago, though I still brag about his spirit protecting me. But domestic abuse is no joke. I am blessed that Roger is much like my father—generous and kind—and thankfully I have never experienced the fits of rage, insane jealousy, mind games, or the vicious cycle of apologies/beatings/more apologies/more beatings that are the hallmarks of abusers. Nevertheless, October is Domestic Abuse Prevention Month, so like the airport signs remind us, "If you see something, say something."

The numbers are staggering. According to domesticviolencestatistics.org, "Every 9 seconds in the U.S. a woman is assaulted or beaten. Around the world, at least one in every three women has been beaten, coerced into sex or otherwise."[16] *The Huffington Post* calls it an epidemic and reports that "women are much more likely to be victims of intimate partner violence with 85 percent . . . of victims being women and 15 percent being men."[17] Yes, men can be and

---

16. domesticviolencestatistics.org
17. www.huffingtonpost.com/2014/10/23/domestic-violence-statistics. In order to access this article, you need a subscription to huffingtonpost.com.

are abused—I saw it one day at the mall, and it wasn't pretty. A woman in rollers and house shoes (already on my "she was wrong for that" list) talked so ugly to her husband, everyone in the store froze and helplessly watched. After loudly and liberally berating and humiliating him, she exhausted herself and left. We all painfully avoided eye contact as he sheepishly headed for the door.

Abuse comes in all shapes and sizes—especially financially, physically, and emotionally. We might ask, *Why don't these people just leave?* Researchers say it takes at least seven episodes before victims get the nerve and means to leave; their abuser cuts them off from family, friends, financial and other support, shatters their self-esteem, and convinces them that they're all alone. Once that's done, the rest is easy. Abusers will often use their children as a weapon for leverage.

This month, consider choosing something from this list to change these sad statistics:

- Talk to your daughter, granddaughter, sister, girlfriend, niece, aunt, grandmother—all the teens and tweens you know—so they don't get caught in this vicious cycle. Adolescent and teen boys are beating their "girlfriends" as early as seventh and eighth grade.

- Wear your "abuse antenna" so if someone's new significant other is just too sweet, too nice, or in too big of a hurry to be in love, you can add a word or two of caution. Lovebirds are usually too smitten to see an abuser until it's too late.

- Don't confront abusers alone or encourage the abused to leave if this might create a more dangerous situation.

- Help victims fund an emergency escape/survival/ sustainability plan to avoid homelessness, and alert their employer so extra workplace safety measures are in place. An "If I can't have you, nobody can" mentality drives so many abusers, and when they have nothing to lose, they can be very dangerous.

Like the scriptures, statistics will say whatever you like if you manipulate them. But all the numbers can't be wrong—domestic abuse *is* an epidemic, and it leaves too many innocents fighting for their lives, dignity, and families simply because they loved the wrong person. We must be vigilant this month and all year, and that's no joke. *Amen.*

Now that you mention it, I will/could/might/won't . . .
Use the space below to jot down some reflections after this reading.

_____

_____

_____

_____

_____

_____

_____

_____

_____

29

Celebrate!

I arrived at my sixty-third year on earth on Tuesday, and I'm celebrating! I have loved birthdays ever since I can remember, so I start celebrating November 1st, so by my real birthday, I'm not just older but wiser. It is my great joy to share this year's *Wisdom Points:*

1. *To be the best, always do and give your best.* This way, you have no regrets. Keep learning, improving, and investing in yourself, because nobody can be a better you than you! Critique, practice, regroup—do whatever it takes to be most excellent, but let excellence be the only standard.

2. *Trust your "first mind" and you won't go wrong.* My Uncle Carey often said, "My first mind told me . . ." and I learned when you start second-guessing yourself or your decisions, that's when you meet disaster. My trusty sidekick Kimberlee puts it this way: "Use the best info you have at the time, decide, and move forward."

3. *Guard your time like you guard your life and your money.* Each week we get 168 hours—whether you squander or invest them wisely, 168 is all you have. So stop saying "yes" to *everything* you're asked, given, or assigned, and understand that "no" is a complete sentence. If you keep doing stuff you don't enjoy, you have less time to do things you love. If you are always busy being busy, blame yourself, then answer these four questions before you take on anything new: (1) Will this matter a year from now? (2) Do I enjoy

it? (3) Would I rather be doing something else? (4) If I die right now, is this something I want to be caught dead doing? If any answer is no, see Wisdom Point #2.

4. *Stop procrastinating.* Go where you've always wanted to go, do what you've always wanted to do, pull out the twelve-year-old bucket list, and work at it like it's a job. Life is short and uncertain, so enjoy the nice towels and real dishes you've been hoarding for "company." Don't think too much of them to use them—nobody else will.

5. *Never underestimate the power of kindness.* Last month I put sticky notes with "You is smart, you is kind, and you is important" on my computer and around the house to affirm and inspire me. These lines from the movie *The Help* gently remind me that I am wondrously and beautifully made, and God is expecting me to bask in all that I have been created to be and to treat others like He treats me—with grace, mercy, patience, and tolerance. Every day.

6. *Take time to admire the clouds and the morning dew today.* Clouds and the morning dew are like comedian Rodney Dangerfield. They just "don't get no respect," yet every day they're "there," being faithful and minding God's business. Now there's a lesson worth learning.

BONUS: Live like you mean it, be blessed, and keep shining! *Amen.*

Now that you mention it, I will/could/might/won't . . .
Use the space below to jot down some reflections after this reading.

_____

_____

_____

_____

_____

30

November Is My Favorite Month!

I love November, yes I do! For one, it's time for my birthday, and I love birthdays better than first graders love cupcakes! And, there are two holidays this month—Veterans Day and Thanksgiving Day. They're sort of cousins, these holidays, and when we celebrate them both, we fully understand that God has blessed us immeasurably.

Back to my birthday. I love telling my new age—sixty-three—because I'm just happy to be alive and know it! I'm a real adult these days, and I know stuff, and you know how much I love to tell you what I know. Today's no different:

1. *Attitude really is everything.* Each day you can choose your attitude—you can be a glass half full or empty, or there's only a cracked, red Solo cup in the trash kind of person—it's up to you. I know there are circumstances, but I still say you can choose—don't let others push your buttons or rain on your parade!

2. *Keep in touch with your friends and mentors.* Don't just call when you need something or when something's wrong. Call to say hello and "I love/appreciate you," and tell these wonderful people what they've meant in your life.

3. *If you take care of your money, your money will take care of you.* Enough said. And teach your children to save/spend/

give equally so they can be self-sufficient in their future. (Of course you can tell them what you like, but they will do what they see you do!)

4. *Make no small plans—dream big.* If you fail, so what? At least you tried, and I would much rather fail trying than to sit around and whine and complain about what didn't happen because I was too scared to try.

5. *Change happens whether you're ready or not and/or whether you notice and acknowledge it or not.* You can prepare, or you can get swept up—either way, things and people change. Those who don't keep up get left behind.

6. *Finally, a word about The Game of Life:* It's not whether you win or lose, it's really how you play the game. If you're in the game, play to win, but play with honor and integrity. If you get mad and take your ball and bat and go home, the Game will go on—with or without you. Remember, what you do today, you must sleep with tonight. Rest easy, be blessed, and keep shining!

Now that you mention it, I will/could/might/won't . . .

Use the space below to jot down some reflections after this reading.

_____

_____

_____

_____

_____

_____

_____

_____

31

Be Thankful Today and Every Day

*I*f all you have today is what you thanked God for yesterday, would you be more thankful today?" In the words of former vice-presidential nominee Sarah Palin, "You betcha!" My new friend, Barbara-Jean, posed this question to me while we were shopping in the airport a couple of weeks ago, and the question still haunts me. Think about all the things we take for granted—clean air, shelter, good health, children, grandchildren—of course the list goes on, but if you think about it, we should/could all thank God more than we do.

On cold nights, I sure thank God that I'm not sleeping outside, but I don't always thank God for the privilege to feel the sunshine on my face or the freedom to admire a spider web in the morning dew or a moonlit night and the beautiful stars overhead. During this season of thanksgiving, let us be ever more mindful that we have so much to be thankful for. If nothing else, thank God for what you don't have or things that could've happened but didn't.

Let this Thanksgiving be your best one, and here are three things you can do to make it so:

1. *Lend a hand.* Instead of stuffing your own turkey this holiday, volunteer at the Salvation Army, the Rescue Mission, or a similar facility, and share your goodwill, best wishes, compassion, and bounty.

2. *Start a gratitude journal.* Each day write down three things and people you're happy to have in your life. Send a note to the folks on your list, and share some kindness with a stranger.

3. *Do what's right, and when you know better, do better.* One of my favorite quotes comes from English anthropologist Thomas Huxley, and he says, "It's not who is right, but what is right, that is of importance." It really isn't important who has the last word. Listen to learn and grow, and do your very best every day in all your endeavors. It'll make you and the world better.

Happy Thanksgiving, and may you and yours be blessed in every way. *Amen.*

Now that you mention it, I will/could/might/won't . . .

Use the space below to jot down some reflections after this reading.

_____

_____

_____

_____

_____

_____

_____

_____

_____

Just Two More Things

Lest We Forget the Reason for the Season

As the month of May comes to a close and Memorial Day quickly approaches, please take time and remember our fallen heroes in a meaningful way. I poignantly remember October 8, 1968, when Vietnam became more than a foreign place we heard about on the evening news. Corporal R. T. Perry from Stanton, Tennessee, my hometown, was killed, and fifty years later, I still remember the tremendous loss we felt along with his family. The devastation was real, and it seemed to permeate every corner of our small church and community. During my first visit to Washington, D.C., I proudly saw his name inscribed on the Vietnam Veterans Memorial and was delighted to see him remembered in this significant way.

Our military families and communities are shattered whenever a "routine" mission becomes anything but routine and soldiers are killed or die in battle for freedoms we often take for granted. Please pause today and pray for our soldiers and their families, because serving often means frequent and extended deployments, life-changing injuries, post-traumatic stress syndrome, higher rates of divorce and suicide, and the list goes on.

The familiar line, "All gave some, but some gave all," must be our clarion call today to (1) pray for peace everywhere,(2) do all we can to elect officials who will study war no more, (3) provide more comprehensively for our widows and orphans, (4) offer intentional support to our first responders and chaplains who care for our families, (5) tell our heroes' stories and keep their memory alive, and (6) celebrate and honor those who made the ultimate sacrifice.

On behalf of a grateful nation, thank you to our soldiers and their families. We owe you a debt we can never repay. *Amen.*

Three Simple Things to Do before Next Year

I have had a glorious day! Here's what I did. I had planned to drive three hours to a funeral, but at 6 a.m. when I woke up, I was three miles and thirty minutes past exhausted. Instead of pushing myself, I turned over and went back to sleep. I woke up three hours later, enjoyed a new magazine, had brunch, saw the matinee of the new Amy Poehler & Tina Fey movie, and laughed out loud, wandered around downtown until 5:30 p.m. and had dinner with my li'l sweet husband. Now I'm lounging in *my* chair. That might not sound like fun to you, but I assure you, today's activity—or lack thereof—probably saved my life. So, in the remaining days this year, here are three things I'm hoping we do and will get done to give January a triumphant start:

1. Be still

2. Declutter

3. Learn the language

First, *be still* and hear. Be still and learn. Be still and reflect. Be still and understand. Be still and plan. The common denominator here? *Be still*. We need to listen and hear God, not just talk. We need quiet time to think creatively and see solutions we won't see if we keep moving. This quote from "Anonymous" says it best: "Intense and important work requires reflection." Being your best you is intensive and important work, so *be still* while the Lord works things out!

Second, *declutter* is a seeing word, and it speaks for itself. Declutter everything—your car, closet, desk, surfaces, mind, heart . . . everything! If you have a spot that attracts clutter, remove, move, or reorganize/organize it. I prescribe to the notion, "A place for everything and everything in its place." That's fine if you don't, but imagine how much time you're wasting "rambling," as my mother called it, for your keys, glasses, homework that needs to be signed, bills that need to be paid, or that hideous brown scarf that goes to the ugly striped tan dress. Multiply that by fifteen minutes, 365 days a year, to see how much time you're wasting. Clean it out, move it out, have a garage sale, take it to the consignment shop—you fill in the blank. But don't keep shuffling stuff around.

Learn the language. Notice I didn't say *learn a new language* (though that is an excellent suggestion). You must learn to manage *you* better. Here's what I mean: "No" is a complete sentence. Use it and mean it. Don't take on anything else until/ unless you let something go. And stop letting folks volunteer you for stuff. My favorite line is, "Cynthia Ann can and will speak for herself." Start doing more of what makes you happy and less of what doesn't. Start early so you won't be late. Arrive alive, and live until you die—we need you!

Make happy memories this holiday season, and make this your best year yet! Be blessed and keep shining!